SING!

Vocal Warm-ups For All Styles

Devised and written by Paul Knight

Order No. AM1009789

Devised and written by Paul Knig...
Edited by Sam Lung.
Music engraved by Camden Music Ser...
Cover and book designed by Chloë Alexande... ...ign.
Audio mixed and mastered by Jonas Persson.
Vocals recorded by Michael Rouse and Lizzie Deane.
Piano recorded by Paul Knight.
Photographs courtesy of Jonas Persson and Fotolia.

To access audio visit:
www.halleonardeurope.com/mylibrary

3573-1984-2315-1085

ISBN: 978-1-78305-783-2

HAL•LEONARD®

Visit Hal Leonard Online at
www.halleonard.com

Contact Us:
Hal Leonard
7777 West Bluemound Road
Milwaukee, WI 53213
Email: info@halleonard.com

In Europe contact:
Hal Leonard Europe Limited
Distribution Centre, Newmarket Road
Bury St Edmunds, Suffolk, IP33 3YB
Email: info@halleonardeurope.com

In Australia contact:
Hal Leonard Australia Pty. Ltd.
4 Lentara Court
Cheltenham, Victoria, 3192 Australia
Email: info@halleonard.com.au

Contents

About the author

Paul Knight has been a vocal coach for over thirty years, working with professional singers in musical theatre, opera, rock, folk and jazz, as well as young and developing voices. He is an established consultant, senior lecturer and vocal coach in many of the UK's leading educational establishments.

Paul studied under the renowned British mezzo-soprano Nancy Evans, famous for roles such as Lucretia and Nancy (from *Albert Herring*) written especially for her by Benjamin Britten.

As a teacher, Paul has a natural ability to inspire and nurture his students. Like athletes, a singer is developed through dedication, exercise, courage and a passion which defies any fear of failure. He has worked with singers of all abilities and even with those who consider themselves to have no abilities! For an individual, all it takes is a readiness to learn and a desire to reach their true potential.

The vocal warm-ups

Singing is fun. It is a fundamental part of our identity. Whatever your ability, whatever style you wish to sing, whatever technique you have been taught, these exercises will strengthen your voice, warm you up safely, extend your abilities, build and connect upper/lower registers and keep your voice protected. They are a springboard to achieving your next level. They will be a guide to finding what every singer searches for — a personal and authentic sound.

Developed over thirty years of vocal exploration, these exercises have been proven by students, collaborators, musical theatre companies, choirs and singing groups. Through teaching varied music cultures around the world Paul Knight has shown the universal use of this method. It works as well in Urdu as it does in English!

How to use the exercises

These exercises have been devised to allow you to create and vary your own warm-up regime. We advise that you first familiarise yourself with all the exercises by listening to the audio demonstrations and following them with the music examples in this book. Once you get the idea, join in!

It's always important to thoroughly warm up your voice before practice, rehearsals and performances, and so you should try to cover as many of these exercises as possible, every time you warm up. The complete set of exercises will take about 45 minutes from start to finish.

If you only have 15 minutes then choose just a few exercises from each section, aiming to cover your full range of techniques. Don't rush and don't strain! Take your time and learn to judge when you're warmed up, active and ready to sing.

Introduction
The Voice

Your voice is an ingenious instrument made up of muscles of the larynx, air, space and the articulators (tongue, teeth, palate, lips). These components interact with each other to produce your unique vocal sound; but you need to keep in mind that a vocalist uses the entire body to sing. This is why body alignment work is so important.

There are three main parts to voice production:

- The **engine** is your breathing tool — lungs and diaphragm.

- The **vibration** comes from the voice box.

- The **resonation** is caused by the throat, mouth and sinus passages.

With these three working together singing is effortless and fun.

Our vocal folds vibrate at about 200 times per second for women and about 100 times per second for men. The higher the pitch, the higher the frequency.

Resonance is also a safety net. By sensing a certain resonance after being trained, a singer knows that the folds are closing in a healthy pattern that creates power without injury.

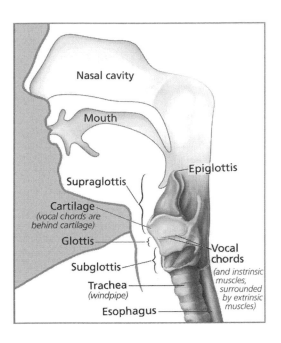

The vocal folds are found within the larynx (voice box) of your throat, made up of a tiny paired muscle, with a mucous lining. The larynx consists of four basic anatomic components: a cartilaginous skeleton, intrinsic muscles, extrinsic muscles and a mucous membrane.

The vocal chords need to be brought together in order to produce sound. If they are too tight or not taut enough the vocal quality suffers.

The larynx must be free to vibrate without excessive tensions from the throat constrictor muscles. Once they are brought together airflow makes them vibrate very quickly through the mucous layer that sits on them.

The key to a good warm up is to ensure that you first achieve good posture. When singing, remember to breathe during natural pauses.

- Keep your head **up** and back of the neck **long**.

- Keep your chin **level**, not forced forward.

- Keep your shoulders **sloping** and **relaxed** — no lifting!

- Keep abdominal and back muscles **relaxed**.

- Keep your knees **loose** and feet slightly apart.

- Keep your toes pointed **forward** with your weight on heels and soles.

The best way of getting the most out of this book...

Smile and Sing!

Section 1
Sing Well

1

Lip trills

For this exercise, you need an even flow of air, soft relaxed lips. The flow must be constant. If you can't get the buzz lift your lips slightly with your fingers, and keep the jaw relaxed.

First, simply make some lip trill sounds, and then add the melody as exampled.

Brr_____   Brr_____   Brr_____

2

Siren unaccompanied

In this exercise, create an 'ng' sound as in 'sing' and take the sound through the folds. Check the 'ng' sound is working by holding your nose for a second. No sound should come out if you are doing this correctly.

Ng_____

Portamento

Taking the siren exercise further, sing this phrase with the jaw relaxed, still to 'ng', sliding downwards.

Ng_____ Ng_____

4

Next, reverse it to slide upwards.
Keep the resonance and volume consistent.

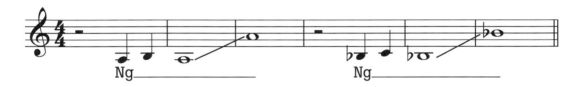

Ng_____ Ng_____

5

Hum changing to 'ahh'

This is a gentle hum. Keep the placement forward, not on the soft palate. You should sense a tickling vibration in the lip and nose area.

Hm_____
Ahh_____

6 'Ooh ahh' changing to 'ee ay'

'Ooh' as in 'hoot', 'ahh' as in 'hark', 'ee' as in 'he', 'ay' as in 'hay'.
Be very clear as to the forward placement of the vowels.

Ooh ahh ooh ahh ooh ahh ooh ahh ooh
Ee ay ee ay ee ay ee ay ee

7 'Mooh mah' changing to 'bree brah'

Feel the tickle of the 'm' on the lips, and roll the 'r' on the 'bree brah' section.

Mooh mah mah_____ mooh mah____
Bree brah brah_____ bree brah____

8 Basic vowels

We will come to the lip and tongue vowels later in the warm up.
For now sing the five basic vowels which are:
'Ah' as in 'father', 'eh' as in 'net', 'ee' as in 'meet', 'oh' as in 'home',
and 'ooh' as in 'blue'.

Ah eh ee oh ooh   Ah eh ee oh ooh

9 Yah

Keep the jaw larynx and tongue relaxed; the 'ah' must have an oval shape. Do not let the corners of the mouth spread.

This exercise can also be sung with the tongue out. However you sing this, you should feel a yawning sensation as you get higher, which opens the back of the throat.

Yah yah   yah   yah   yah   yah   yah   yah

10 No-ah

This exercise is an extension of 'yah' and demands a smooth transition between the 'oh' and the 'ah'. There must be no 'w'. It is not 'Nowah'!

No - ah___   no - ah___   no - ah___   no

no - ah___   no - ah___   no - ah___   no

The mix

This is both a vocal chord event and a head resonance event.
Keep the air flow consistent and do not push the chest voice.
You need to introduce some nasality to the voice to warm up the mix.

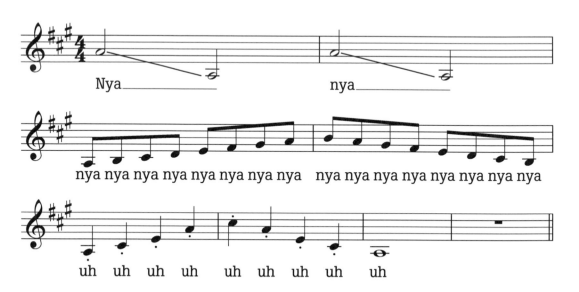

Nya_____ nya_____

nya nya nya nya nya nya nya nya   nya nya nya nya nya nya nya nya

uh   uh   uh   uh   uh   uh   uh   uh   uh

Sing 'nya' as a slur from the top down and as a scale, followed by 'uh' (a neutral vowel which stops the larynx from rising). This will help in establishing the muscle memory of the mix voice. The resonance which starts in the mouth will move to the soft palate, causing you to experience 'split resonance' where you feel as though you are in chest and head voice simultaneously. The intention is to be able to move through these registers seamlessly.

Section 2
Sing Low

12 Mad
Make a hard 'a' sound and go deep into the growl of the voice.

Mad_____   Mad_____   Mad_____   etc.

13 Take, talk, tick, taa
Even though these octave scales are going down to your lower register, think upwards, counter-intuitively, and don't collapse onto the notes.

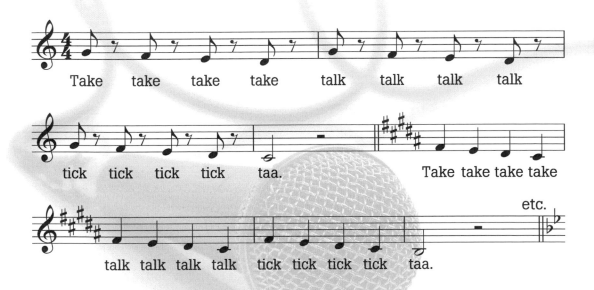

Take   take   take   take   talk   talk   talk   talk

tick   tick   tick   tick   taa.   Take take take take

talk talk talk talk   tick tick tick tick   taa.   etc.

Section 3
Sing Supported

Have you noticed how babies can breathe and scream to great effect? Without even thinking about it, they use their full breathing mechanism! To breathe for singing we need to use the whole of our lungs to make as much air available as possible. By using the natural motion of the diaphragm and abdominals we control the amount of air that is exhaled.

The diaphragm is an involuntary muscle, rather like your heart. You cannot really control it. Let it take care of itself. If you imagine lengthening and widening your body, you are engaging your *trapezii* (large triangular muscles extending over the back of the neck and shoulders). Engage your pelvic floor (as done in pilates), and for balance you must also engage your lats (*latissimus dorsi*).

A useful exercise is to imagine you are holding ski sticks and push your elbows down. After you have found your lats, try finding your *quadratus lumborum*. These muscles sit slightly deeper. Do not engage support before you breathe in as this will lead to constriction.

Release is of equal importance. Let go completely. Do not tighten. For women who 'belt' remember you need much less air – almost as if you are coming off your air flow, and the support feels as though it is much higher.

14 Va, vay, vee, voh, voo

Use more consonant than vowel in this exercise, and do not push the air through. As you go higher you will feel your support strengthen.

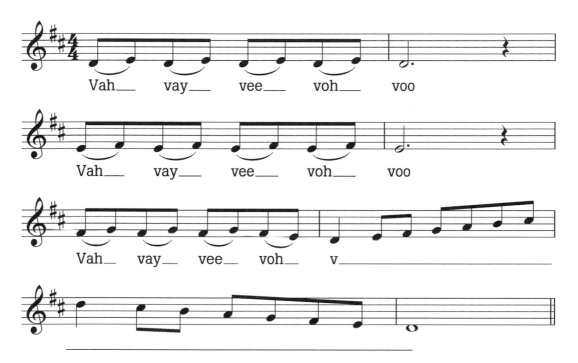

Vah__ vay__ vee__ voh__ voo

Vah__ vay__ vee__ voh__ voo

Vah__ vay__ vee__ voh__ v_____

15 'Ooh' opening to 'ahh'

This exercise requires a steady air flow. Too much space between the vocal chords will create a breathy sound. Keep your shoulders relaxed and down. Use this exercise to practice controlling the speed, quantity and consistency of airflow released.

Ooh_____ ahh_____

Rolled 'rr'

If this is a challenge, don't get stressed!

Firstly, keep the tongue loose and start making short trilling 'trr' and 'drr' sounds. It doesn't matter how short they are — they are in the right placement. Now begin to lose the 't' and the 'd', making a rolling 'rr' sound. This will take time. Persevere. It will happen!

Rr_____

See-aw

In this exercise, stop the sound after each short phrase but do not take a breath. Maintain your support, and think of each two-note phrase as a fresh start.

See-aw see-aw   see-aw see-aw   see-aw see-aw   see-aw

Staccato

Be careful not to sing this 'on the voice'. Almost suspend the breath and open the rib cage. Practising songs with staccato helps to reveal where you need to make better placement choices, highlighting what you need to work on. A true staccato sound is clear and not guttural. It emphasises the importance of the correct attack on a note.

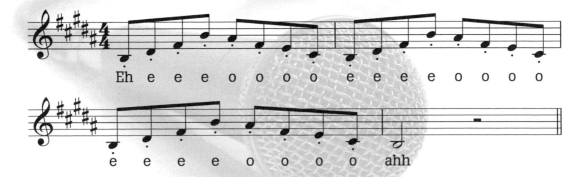

Eh e e e o o o o   e e e e o o o o

e e e e o o o o ahh

19 Legato intervals

This will take you through your entire range. You must ensure that when you return to the bottom note it is correctly placed each time. There must be a smooth connection from note to note, from start to finish. Use various vowels of your choice. Listen out for aspirations or glottal stops. Glottal stops give a hard edge to the sound and are caused by the throat slightly gripping the vocal chords together. Relaxation is the vocal antidote!

20 Faster legato intervals

Maintain exactly the same focus and support as in the previous exercise, but with a greater facility in the scalic passages.

Section 4
Sing Long

21 T'adoro

This is a controlled crescendo exercise (gradually getting louder) over eight beats. Start quietly and build.

T'a - do - - - ro T'a -

22 Maria

This is a controlled diminuendo exercise (gradually getting softer), demanding a solid support. Start loudly and drink the sound in as you get quieter.

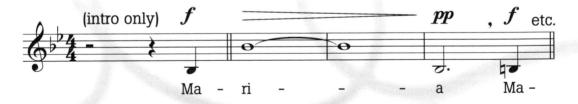

Ma - ri - - - a Ma -

Count from 1 to 30

Count from 1 to 30 on one note, evenly, articulately
and **without getting faster**.

At first you may need to take a surprise* breath somewhere during the exercise,
but eventually you will connect the three main elements of airflow, vocal chord
co-ordination and vocal resonance.

*A surprise breath is not a shallow breath. It is deeply rooted, and equivalent to
the breath you would take on being surprised at how wonderful something was —
a 'wow' moment. It is not the high chest breath or gasp that you would take
when shocked.*

Section 5
Sing Freely

24 **Tongue exercises** unaccompanied
This is an 'l' exercise.
The tongue is a large muscle which extends to the back of the throat.

The neck muscles must remain relaxed as it will affect the way you use your tongue. How you use your tongue affects your sound. If the tongue pulls up too much it pulls the larynx up and out of position, If the tongue presses down it pushes the larynx lower, but still out of position. This gives your vocal folds a hard time! A tight tongue can muffle the sound and affect the warmth of your tone and can make the singer push the voice.

a Put the tip of your tongue between the lips and then swallow.

b Put half the tongue between the lips and then swallow.

c Put the full tongue out fully, as far as you can, and then swallow.

If the last exercise is too difficult concentrate on **(a)** and **(b)** until the tongue is more relaxed. This releases the muscles that surround the larynx.

Next, pull out the tongue and imagine a clock face.
Point the tongue to:
a 12 o'clock ⬆
b 3 o'clock ➡
c 9 o'clock ⬅
d 6 o'clock ⬇

If you have a mirror, look into it. Pull your tongue all the way out and sing a siren going up. Do not let the tongue gradually return to the mouth. That is a sign of a tense tongue.

Lay lee lee

Put into action what we have just practised in the previous exercise, keeping the tongue light and relaxed. 'Lay lee lee' on the way up, 'lee lay lay' on the way down.

Lay lee lee lay lee lee   lay lee lee lay lee lee   lay lee lee lay lee lee

lay lee lee lay   Lee lay lay lee lay lay   lee lay lay lee lay lay

lee lay lay lee lay lay   lee lay lay lee

Scales

Sing this exercise to 'ma', 'me' and 'maw'.
The last two bars are staccato and stop the diaphragm from tensing.
This is to be sung in one breath.

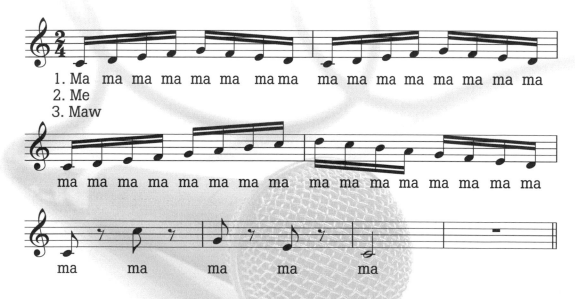

1. Ma ma ma ma ma ma ma ma   ma ma ma ma ma ma ma ma
2. Me
3. Maw

ma ma ma ma ma ma ma ma   ma ma ma ma ma ma ma ma

ma   ma   ma   ma   ma

27 Long / short

This exercise does not demand a lot of air. Keep the mouth relaxed and focus on the soft palette.

You must establish a strong support. This exercise helps with natural pauses and designated rests, encouraging optimal breath control. Ensure that the short note is connected to the breath. Aim to sing lightly — if the sound is too 'airy' then too much air is escaping, and this will make it harder.

Ah___ ah___ ah___ ah ah___ ah___ ah___ ah

ah___ ah___ ah___ ah ha ha ha ha hah

28 Delay

This exercise incorporates scales, crescendo, vocal stamina and attention to vowels.

Be aware of the diphthong — two vowel sounds occurring in the same vowel. Use the target vowel (the sound at the front of the word) to sing on and complete the rest quickly at the end of the note. Do not allow the sounds to 'migrate' — where you move gradually between the vowels. This exercise is to be sung in one breath.

De - lay___

Vowel placement

When it comes to vowel exercises remember that there are lip vowels, as exampled by the following words: hoot, hook, hoe, haw, hot and hark.

Then there are tongue vowels, as exampled by these words: hut, her, have, head, hay, hit and he. Get to know in detail the positioning of each of these vowels. Practise saying the words without the consonants and allow the vowels to link smoothly. Now sing them lightly on this arpeggio, first with lip vowels.

Once you have done that, use the tongue vowels on this arpeggio.

Grazie

Italian is a great language for singing in a clear and open way. Use the word 'grazie' to sing the melody as phrased in the example, with stops but NOT breaths at the end of each phrase — complete the exercise in one breath.

Section 6
Sing Clearly

These next exercises are to improve articulation. They can be tricky at first, so persevere and listen carefully to what you are singing.

Make sure you are singing the correct words! Have fun with them...

Consonants unaccompanied

Consonants are formed by the mouth. If over-emphasised they can cause you to push out too much air and tense the muscles in your throat and mouth.

We need to understand whether a consonant is voiced or unvoiced. If a consonant is voiced there is a vibration of the vocal fold.

'P' is an unvoiced sound and 'b' is a voiced sound, but note that with this example both sounds are produced in the same place at the front of the mouth.

Speak out the consonants and you will sense them gradually placed further back in the mouth with the final pair being produced in the throat.

p p p p p p, b b b b b b (x3) *then* **p b p b p b p b**

v v v v v v, f f f f f f (x3) *then* **v f v f v f v f**

*th th th th th th, **th th th th th th (x3) *then* ***th **th th th th th th th**
(* *as in* they)   (** *as in* thirty)

d d d d d d, t t t t t t (x3) *then* **d t d t d t d t**

z z z z z z, s s s s s s (x3) *then* **z s z s z s z s**

*g g g g g g, sh sh sh sh sh sh (x3) *then* **g sh g sh g sh g sh**
(* *as in* genre)

j j j j j j, ch ch ch ch ch ch (x3) *then* **j ch j ch j ch j ch**

*g g g g g g, k k k k k k (x3) *then* **g k g k g k g k**
(* *as in* good)

33 Plain bun, plum bun

In this exercise focus on the plosive (practised in the previous exercise) and the placement of 'm' and 'n'.

Plain   bun   plum   bun   plain   plum   bun

34 Sister Susie

Beware of suffering from superfluous sibilance!

Sis – ter Su – sie sit-ting in a shoe shine

shop. All day long she sits and shines, all day long she

shines and sits. Sis – ter Su – sie sit-ting in a shoe shine

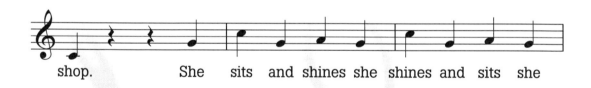

shop. She sits and shines she shines and sits she

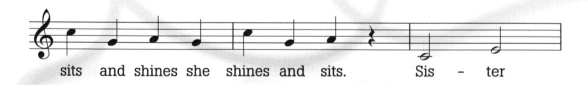

sits and shines she shines and sits. Sis – ter

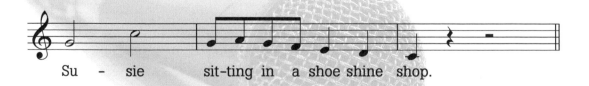

Su – sie sit-ting in a shoe shine shop.

Numbers

This is an exercise to make you think! Once you have learned it you can keep your brain active by choosing a number to omit in the sequence. It really keeps you focused!

1 1 2 1   1 2   3 2 1   1 2 3 4   3 2 1   1 2 3 4

5 4 3 2 1   1 2   3 4 5 6 5 4 3 2   1   1 2 3 4 5 6

7 6 5 4 3 2 1   1 2 3 4 5 6 7 8   7 6 5 4 3 2   1

8 8 7 8   8 7   6 7 8   8 7 6 5   6 7 8   8 7 6 5

4 5 6 7 8   8 7   6 5 4 3 4 5 6 7   8   8 7 6 5 4 3

2 3 4 5 6 7 8   8 7 6 5 4 3 2 1   2 3 4 5 6 7 8

Section 7
Sing Out!

In these final exercises feel the shape and natural rise and fall of the phrase. Remember no two artists phrase the same passage in exactly the same way. Choose some phrases to sing full out and other phrases to sing quietly.

Explore the qualities of your voice as each phrase rises up in key. Put into action your tuning, your support, your released tongue, your **voiced** and **unvoiced** consonants and your ability to crescendo and diminuendo.

- Give yourself permission to sing out.

- It is good for you to be heard.

- It is good for you to be seen.

- It is good for you to **SMILE** and **SING!**

36 Il mio dolce amore

Il mio dol-ce a - mo - - - re

37 I can sing

I can sing_____
dance_____
move_____
laugh_____

38 Bella signora

Bel - la sig - no - - - - ra.

Bel - la_ sig - no - ra.   Bel - la_ sig - no - ra.

39 Signor Pieta

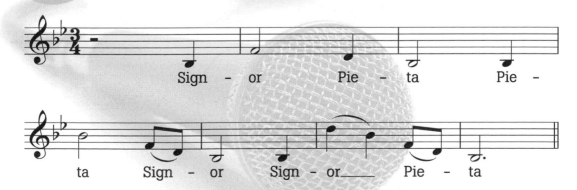

Sign - or   Pie - ta   Pie -

ta   Sign - or   Sign - or____   Pie - ta